TULSA CITY-COUNTY LIBRARY

MRJC

FEB - - 2019

D1304005

BEAKED BATTLERS

Ornithopods

Clare Hibbert

Enslow Publishing
101 W. 23rd Street
Suite 240
New York, NY 10011
USA
enslow.com

Published in 2019 by Enslow Publishing, LLC
101 W. 23rd Street, Suite 240, New York, NY 10011

Copyright © 2019 by Enslow Publishing, LLC

All rights reserved.

No part of this book may be reproduced by any means without the written permission of the publisher.

Cataloging-in-Publication Data

Names: Hibbert, Clare.
Title: Beaked Battlers: Ornithopods / Clare Hibbert.
Description: New York : Enslow Publishing, 2019. | Series: Dino explorers | Includes glossary and index.
Identifiers: ISBN 9780766099906 (pbk.) | ISBN 9780766099890 (library bound) | ISBN 9781978500037 (6 pack.) | ISBN 9780766099913 (ebook)
Subjects: LCSH: Ornithischia--Juvenile literature. | Dinosaurs--Juvenile literature.
Classification: LCC QE862.O65 H53 2019 | DDC 567.914--dc23

Printed in the United States of America

To Our Readers: We have done our best to make sure all website addresses in this book were active and appropriate when we went to press. However, the author and the publisher have no control over and assume no liability for the material available on those websites or on any websites they may link to. Any comments or suggestions can be sent by email to customerservice@enslow.com.

Excerpts and articles have been reproduced with the permission of the copyright holders.

Photo Credits:
Key: b-bottom, t-top, c-center, l-left, r-right
Stefano Azzalin: 6–7, 11t, 26c; Juan Calle: 17cr; Mat Ed: profile box icons, cover, cover cl, 1, 1cl, 8–9, 10–11, 12–13, 14–15, 18–19, 20–21, 22–23, 24–25, 26tl, 26bl, 26br, 27tr, 27bl, 31br; Rudolf Farkas: 16–17; Kunal Kundu: 17tl, 27tl, 31bl; Shutterstock: cover bl/1bl/20bl/27c Elenarts, 9t Linda Bucklin, 13r CTR Photos, 18tr Adwo, 23br/17br Warpaint, 28cr gorosan, 29tl Alessandro De Maddalena, 29cr ZayacSK; Wikimedia Commons: cover cr/1cr/6c Carol Abraczinskas, Paul C Sereno/ZooKeys, cover br/1br/6br/26tr Daderot/University of California Museum of Paleontology, cover bc/1bc/22c Conty and Ballista/Oxford University Museum, 9bl Joseph Smit/biodiversitylibrary.org, 11cr Aimé Rutot, 14cr FunkMonk, 18bl William Diller Matthew, 24l UNC Sea Grant College Program, 25t Tim Evanson/Museum of the Rockies.

CONTENTS

The Dinosaur Age

Dinosaurs appeared around 225 million years ago (mya) and ruled the land for over 160 million years. At the same time (the Mesozoic Era), marine reptiles and pterosaurs ruled the oceans and skies.

This family tree shows when various dinosaurs appeared and and how they were related. As new fossils are found, paleontologists often change their minds about the groupings.

Dinosaurs suddenly died out 65 mya, along with marine reptiles, pterosaurs, and many other animals. A huge meteorite probably hit Earth, throwing up dust that blocked out the Sun for months.

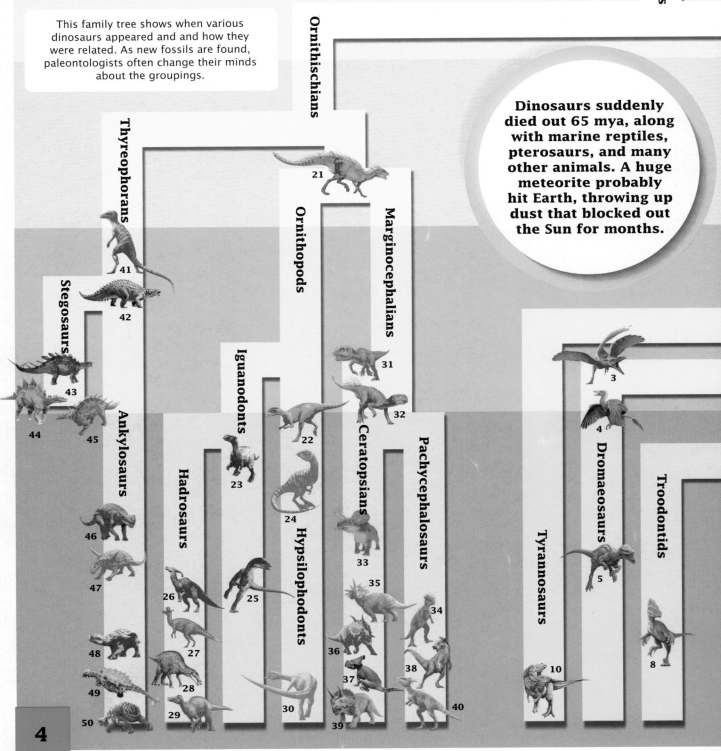

Dinosaurs

Ornithischians

Thyreophorans

Stegosaurs

Ankylosaurs

Hadrosaurs

Iguanodonts

Ornithopods

Hypsilophodonts

Marginocephalians

Ceratopsians

Pachycephalosaurs

Tyrannosaurs

Dromaeosaurs

Troodontids

4

KEY

1. *Herrerasaurus*
2. *Allosaurus*
3. *Archaeopteryx*
4. *Microraptor*
5. *Deinonychus*
6. *Spinosaurus*
7. *Giganotosaurus*
8. *Troodon*
9. *Therizinosaurus*
10. *Tyrannosaurus*

11. *Melanorosaurus*
12. *Plateosaurus*
13. *Mamenchisaurus*
14. *Brachiosaurus*
15. *Amargasaurus*
16. *Nigersaurus*
17. *Sauroposeidon*
18. *Argentinosaurus*
19. *Saltasaurus*
20. *Rapetosaurus*

21. *Heterodontosaurus*
22. *Hypsilophodon*
23. *Iguanodon*
24. *Leaellynasaura*
25. *Gasparinisaura*
26. *Parasaurolophus*
27. *Lambeosaurus*
28. *Shantungosaurus*
29. *Edmontosaurus*
30. *Thescelosaurus*

31. *Yinlong*
32. *Psittacosaurus*
33. *Zuniceratops*
34. *Stegoceras*
35. *Styracosaurus*
36. *Achelousaurus*
37. *Protoceratops*
38. *Pachycephalosaurus*
39. *Triceratops*
40. *Stygimoloch*

41. *Scutellosaurus*
42. *Scelidosaurus*
43. *Tuojiangosaurus*
44. *Stegosaurus*
45. *Kentrosaurus*
46. *Minmi*
47. *Sauropelta*
48. *Edmontonia*
49. *Euoplocephalus*
50. *Ankylosaurus*

Saurischians

Theropods

Allosaurs

Sauropods

Prosauropods

Diplodocids

Spinosaurs

Titanosaurs

Therizinosaurs

Triassic
251–206 mya

Jurassic
206–145 mya

Cretaceous
145–65 mya

1

11

12

2

13

14

16

7

47

15

17

18

19

20

9

Heterodontosaurus

One of the earliest ornithischians, or bird-hipped, dinosaurs, *Heterodontosaurus* lived in South Africa about 195 mya. Its name means "different-toothed lizard." Unlike most reptiles, it had teeth of several different shapes.

Tooth Types

Heterodontosaurus's square cheek teeth were used for grinding and chewing. At the front of its beak-like, horny snout, it had smaller front teeth for snipping off plant stems. Finally, it had a pair of curved tusks.

Heterodontosaurus probably used its tusks to show off to rivals.

This is a cast of the *Heterodontosaurus* skeleton discovered in 1966.

Discoveries

The first *Heterodontosaurus* fossil was a skull, discovered in 1961. Five years later another skull was found—this time attached to an almost perfect skeleton. Since then, more finds have surfaced. The most complete skeleton was found in 2005, but it could not be excavated because it had fossilized in such hard rock.

PERIOD	TRIASSIC	JURASSIC	CRETACEOUS	AGE OF MAMMALS

MILLIONS OF YEARS AGO

195

251   206   145   65   present

Name: *Heterodontosaurus*
(Het-er-uh-DON-tuh-SAWR-us)
Family: Heterodontisauridae
Height: 1 foot (0.3 m)
Length: 3.9 feet (1.2 m)
Weight: 5.7 pounds (2.6 kg)

DINOSAUR PROFILE

Heterodontosaurus could run fast to escape predators.

One of its later Chinese cousins had feathers, so *Heterodontosaurus* probably had them, too.

Heterodontosaurus had five digits on its "hands"—good for grasping—and four on its "feet."

Heterodontosaurus was a plant-eater, but it may have also fed on insects.

Hypsilophodon

During the Early Cretaceous, the Isle of Wight, a small island off the south coast of England, was home to a small, fast-moving dinosaur called *Hypsilophodon*. It browsed on tough plants such as ferns and cycads and probably lived in herds for safety.

Threatening Theropods

The main hunters in *Hypsilophodon*'s habitat were *Baryonyx*, *Eotyrannus*, and *Neovenator*. *Baryonyx* had a narrow jaw and was probably a specialist fish eater. *Eotyrannus* was a pony-sized tyrannosaur. The top predator was a 25-foot- (7.6-m) long allosaur called *Neovenator* ("new hunter").

Hypsilophodon's short, beak-like snout was ideal for snapping off low-growing plants.

The landscape was hot and usually dry. Any rain caused flash floods.

PERIOD	TRIASSIC	JURASSIC	CRETACEOUS	AGE OF MAMMALS

128

| MILLIONS OF YEARS AGO | 251 | 206 | 145 | 65 | present |

Name: *Hypsilophodon* (Hip-sih-LO-fuh-don)
Family: Hypsilophodontidae
Height: 2 feet (0.6 m)
Length: 5.9 feet (1.8 m)
Weight: 44 pounds (20 kg)

DINOSAUR PROFILE

Hypsilophodon, like *Heterodontosaurus* (pages 6–7), was bipedal. It was one of the earliest ornithischians.

Hypsilophodon had a stiff tail that stuck out behind for balance.

Hypsilophodon had a lightweight skeleton that helped it to be fast-moving.

Different Postures

Many 19th-century reconstructions of *Hypsilophodon* wrongly showed it on four legs, like a lizard. There was also a theory that this dinosaur used its grasping hands to move around in the trees. Today, paleontologists agree that *Hypsilophodon* was a ground dweller.

A quadrupedal *Hypsilophodon* (left) and a kangaroo-like one (right).

Iguanodon

Iguanodon walked on all fours, with its body and tail parallel to the ground.

The large plant-eater *Iguanodon* roamed across Europe and North America during the Early and Mid Cretaceous. More than 25 species are known. *Iguanodon* moved in herds for protection against predators such as *Deinonychus*.

Some experts think that *Iguanodon* may have had cheek pouches for storing food.

Iguanodon sometimes reared up to reach for food or look for danger.

Eating Technique

Iguanodon had a toothless beak for breaking off tough ferns and other plants, and wide cheek teeth for mashing and pulping plant matter. The teeth were similar to a modern-day iguana's (*Iguanodon* means "iguana tooth").

Iguanodon's tail stuck out stiffly behind it.

Early Finds

Iguanodon was only the second dinosaur to be named (the first was *Megalosaurus*). The first fossils were a few teeth from southern England. The most spectacular finds came from a coal mine at Bernissart in Belgium. Nearly 40 *Iguanodon* skeletons were uncovered there in 1878.

Iguanodon had a vicious thumb spike to stab at would-be attackers.

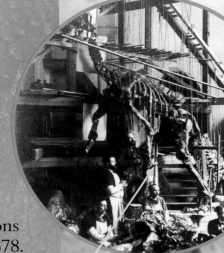

An *Iguanodon* skeleton from Bernissart, Belgium, being mounted for display

PERIOD	TRIASSIC	JURASSIC	CRETACEOUS	AGE OF MAMMALS
			121	
MILLIONS OF YEARS AGO	251	206	145	65 present

Name: *Iguanodon* (Ig-WAN-oh-don)
Family: Iguanodontidae
Height: 10.7 feet (3.3 m)
Length: 33 feet (10 m)
Weight: 3.4 tons (3.1 t)

DINOSAUR PROFILE

Leaellynasaura

Large-eyed *Leaellynasaura* lived about 110 mya. During the winter months this plant-eater had to cope with total darkness and cooler temperatures because its forest habitat was inside the Antarctic Circle.

The Antarctic Circle was warmer in the Cretaceous than it is today.

Like all hypsilophodonts, *Leaellynasaura* was small and speedy. It moved around on two legs.

Leaellynasaura relied on its excellent eyesight to look out for predators.

Leaellynasaura's long tail contained more than 70 vertebrae.

110

Name: *Leaellynasaura*
(Lee-ELL-in-ah-SAWR-ah)
Family: Hypsilophontidae
Height: 2 feet (0.6 m)
Length: 5.9 feet (1.8 m)
Weight: 44 pounds (20 kg)

DINOSAUR PROFILE

Dinosaur Cove

Leaellynasaura was discovered in 1989 at Dinosaur Cove in Victoria, on the coast of southeast Australia. The sand and mudstone cliffs there formed in the Early Cretaceous. Other dinosaurs found at the site include another two-legged plant-eater, *Atlascopcosaurus*, and a small theropod called *Timimus*.

This image of *Leaellynasaura* was created for an Australian postage stamp.

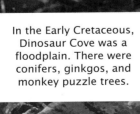

In the Early Cretaceous, Dinosaur Cove was a floodplain. There were conifers, ginkgos, and monkey puzzle trees.

Keeping Warm

During the Early Cretaceous, the southern tip of Australia fell within the Antarctic Circle. Temperatures were milder than they are today. However, there still would have been less food during the long winter months when that part of the Earth was facing away from the Sun. There is no evidence that *Leaellynasaura* hibernated, but it may have sheltered in burrows.

Gasparinisaura

Speedy little plant-eater *Gasparinisaura* lived in Argentina around 85 mya. It belonged to the same family as the much larger *Iguanodon* (pages 10–11) and fed on tough vegetation, including conifers and cycads.

Daily Grind

Stones called gastroliths have been found with *Gasparinisaura*. Its stomach could contain as many as 140 stones, each less than 0.4 inches (1 cm) across. Plant matter was ground up as it passed between the stones, making it easier to digest.

Tiny *Gasparinisaura* skeletons are on display in Denmark.

Large eyes, high on its head, gave *Gasparinisaura* good all-around vision, so that it could spot danger.

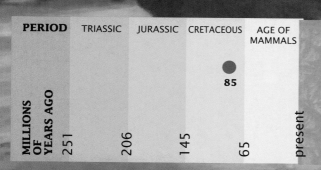

PERIOD	TRIASSIC	JURASSIC	CRETACEOUS	AGE OF MAMMALS
MILLIONS OF YEARS AGO	251	206	145	65	present

85

Name: *Gasparinisaura*
(Gas-pah-reen-ee-SAWR-uh)
Family: Iguanodontidae
Height: 2.6 feet (0.8 m)
Length: 5.6 feet (1.7 m)
Weight: 29 pounds (13 kg)

DINOSAUR PROFILE

Living with Giants

Gasparinisaura fossils come from rock that formed in what is now Patagonia, Argentina, during the Late Cretaceous. Other species found nearby include the titanosaurs *Argentinosaurus*, *Saltasaurus,* and *Antarctosaurus*, and the theropods *Aucasaurus* and *Abelisaurus*.

Gasparinisaura shared its habitat with some of the largest ever sauropods, *Argentinosaurus*.

Gasparinisaura probably had a thumb spike like its cousin, *Iguanodon*.

Parasaurolophus

One of the hadrosaurs, or duck-billed, dinosaurs, herbivorous *Parasaurolophus* lived across North America around 75 mya. It was thought to be a close relative of another hadrosaur, *Saurolophus* ("crested lizard"). *Parasaurolophus* means "like *Saurolophus*."

The crest made its calls travel further.

Skull Features

Saurolophus's crest was mostly solid, while *Parasaurolophus*'s was hollow. It had tubes leading to and from the nostrils and amplified the dinosaur's calls (made them louder). *Parasaurolophus*'s closest relative was the large Asian hadrosaur *Charonosaurus*.

Parasaurolophus went up on two legs to run or look out for danger.

Parasaurolophus's short, stout legs helped it to push through thick undergrowth.

Parasaurolophus grazed on all fours.

Hot Head

Some paleontologists believe that *Parasaurolophus*'s crest helped it to keep its body temperature steady. It could have soaked up heat during the daytime to keep *Parasaurolophus* warm at night. Another possibility is that *Parasaurolophus* could lose excess body heat through its crest, to stop it becoming too hot.

Including the crest, *Parasaurolophus*'s skull could be more than 6.6 feet (2 m) long, depending on the species.

Parasaurolophus communicated with members of the herd to warn of predators or to attract a mate.

The crest grew larger with age. It may have looked different in males and females.

PERIOD	TRIASSIC	JURASSIC	CRETACEOUS	AGE OF MAMMALS	
MILLIONS OF YEARS AGO	251	206	145	65	present

75

Name: *Parasaurolophus*
(Par-ah-SAWR-OL-uh-fus)
Family: Hadrosauridae
Height: 12 feet (3.7 m)
Length: 36 feet (11 m)
Weight: 2.8 tons (2.5 t)

DINOSAUR PROFILE

Lambeosaurus

All the hollow-crested hadrosaurs are known as the lambeosaurines, after *Lambeosaurus*. Like *Parasaurolophus* (pages 16–17), *Lambeosaurus* lived in North America around 75 mya. It was named after Lawrence Lambe, the Canadian paleontologist who first studied it.

Dinosaur Park Formation

The layer of rock in Alberta, Canada, where *Lambeosaurus* was discovered is called the Dinosaur Park Formation. It contains other hadrosaurs, including *Parasaurolophus* and *Corythosaurus*, pachycephalosaurs such as *Stegoceras*, ceratopsians including *Styracosaurus,* and ankylosaurs such as *Edmontonia* and *Euoplocephalus*.

The crest looked like an ax-head.

Lambeosaurus had more than 100 teeth in its cheeks for chewing.

The American paleontologist Barnum Brown excavated the first *Corythosaurus* specimen in 1912.

Complicated Cousin

Corythosaurus, whose name means "helmeted lizard," was the same size as *Lambeosaurus* and lived in the same habitat. The main difference was the complex passages inside its crest. These would have turned any calls *Corythosaurus* made into very deep, low-pitched sounds that could travel great distances.

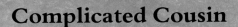

PERIOD	TRIASSIC	JURASSIC	CRETACEOUS	AGE OF MAMMALS

MILLIONS OF YEARS AGO

251 206 145 65 present

75

Name: *Lambeosaurus*
(LAM-be-uh-SAWR-us)
Family: Hadrosauridae
Height: 13 feet (4 m)
Length: 32 feet (10 m)
Weight: 5 tons (4.5 t)

DINOSAUR PROFILE

The crest may have been used for display, to amplify sounds, and perhaps even to improve *Lambeosaurus*'s sense of smell.

The plant-eater lived in swampy forests.

Lambeosaurus moved around on four legs or two, so it could reach plants growing at different levels.

Shantungosaurus

Not all duck-billed dinosaurs had a crest. *Shantungosaurus*, one of the largest known hadrosaurs, did not have one. It may have had its own method of making its calls distinctive—an inflatable flap of skin near its nostrils that made sounds.

From Shandong

Shantungosaurus means "Shandong lizard," after the province of eastern China where the dinosaur was discovered. It was named in 1973 and five incomplete skeletons have been dug up to date. When *Shantungosaurus* was alive, the environment was a humid floodplain.

Shantungosaurus has knocked over a predatory *Tarbosaurus* with a powerful swipe of its tail.

PERIOD	TRIASSIC	JURASSIC	CRETACEOUS	AGE OF MAMMALS
MILLIONS OF YEARS AGO	251	206	145	65	present

74

Name: *Shantungosaurus*
(Shan-TUNG-o-SAWR-us)
Family: Hadrosauridae
Height: 16.4 feet (5 m)
Length: 51 feet (15.5 m)
Weight: 18 tons (16 t)

DINOSAUR PROFILE

The 5.3-foot (1.6-m) skull ended with a toothless beak. The jaws contained 1,500 tiny teeth.

Good Mothers

One of the best-known duck-bills is *Maiasaura*, whose name means "good mother lizard." *Maiasaura* nurseries have been uncovered, and experts believe that this dinosaur incubated its eggs and may even have cared for its young. Perhaps other hadrosaurs also did this.

Shantungosaurus hatchlings may have been too helpless to find food for themselves.

Hadrosaurs laid round eggs.

Edmontosaurus

One of the largest hadrosaurs, *Edmontosaurus* lived at the end of the dinosaur age. It was the North American cousin of Asian *Shantungosaurus* (pages 20–21). It was named after Edmonton, capital city of Alberta, the Canadian province where *Edmontosaurus* was found.

Walking and Running

Usually, herbivorous *Edmontosaurus* walked on all fours. It could run at speeds faster than 31 mph (50 km/h), typically on two legs but sometimes on four. Running was its best way to escape predators. One *Edmontosaurus* was found with a theropod bite on its tail bone.

Edmontosaurus had a small crest, or comb. It was made of skin and scales, not bone.

Edmontosaurus's backbone was held horizontally above the hip bone.

PERIOD	TRIASSIC	JURASSIC	CRETACEOUS	AGE OF MAMMALS
MILLIONS OF YEARS AGO	251	206	145	65 · present

70

Name: *Edmontosaurus*
(Ed-MON-tuh-SAWR-us)
Family: Hadrosauridae
Height: 11.5 feet (3.5 m)
Length: 39 feet (12 m)
Weight: 4.4 tons (4 t)

DINOSAUR PROFILE

The long, narrow skull ended in a beaky mouth.

Paleontologists have been able to study fossilized *Edmontosaurus* skin.

No Limits

Some experts think that *Edmontosaurus* could have grown as large as *Shantungosaurus*—if an individual managed to live long enough. Their evidence is a 25-foot (7.6-m) *Edmontosaurus* tail. Unfortunately most *Edmontosaurus* seem to have died before reaching that size, because of predators, disease, or some other disaster.

As *Edmontosaurus* grew older, its skull became longer and flatter.

Thescelosaurus

The first *Thescelosaurus* fossil was found in 1891, but then stored in a crate and ignored for more than 20 years. When it was finally studied, it was named *Thescelosaurus neglectus* (*Thescelosaurus* means "wonderful lizard" and *neglectus* means "ignored").

Willo's Heart of Stone

In 2000, experts in North Carolina, introduced the most complete *Thescelosaurus* skeleton. They called it Willo and claimed it had a heart. Fossilized hearts are extremely rare because they are made up of soft tissue. Unfortunately, experts now think the "heart" is just a lump of rock that formed during fossilization.

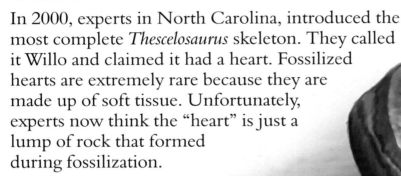

Thescelosaurus's thighs were longer than its calves. (Fast-running ornithopods had the opposite—longer calves and shorter thighs.)

Paleontologists thought this dark ring inside Willo's chest might be its heart.

PERIOD	TRIASSIC	JURASSIC	CRETACEOUS	AGE OF MAMMALS
MILLIONS OF YEARS AGO	251	206	145	65 ⬤ 66 / present

Name: *Thescelosaurus* (Theh-SEL-uh-SAWR-us)
Family: Thescelosauridae
Height: 5.7 feet (1.7 m)
Length: 12.3 feet (3.7 m)
Weight: 550 pounds (250 kg)

DINOSAUR PROFILE

Just Plants?

Thescelosaurus has been found across North America, from Canada to New Mexico. It lived on floodplains, along riverbanks, and beside lakes. It had the leaf-shaped teeth at the back of its mouth that most herbivores have. However, it also had short, pointy front teeth, which might mean that it also ate some meat.

This *Thescelosaurus* skeleton came from the Hell Creek Formation in Montana.

Thescelosaurus's small front teeth suggest that it might have been an omnivore.

Thescelosaurus ran upright on two legs.

Fun Facts

Now that you have discovered some amazing ornithopods, boost your knowledge with these 10 quick facts about them!

Fruitadens was the smallest heterodontosaurid. It was just 27.5 inches (70 cm) long and lived in Late Jurassic North America.

More than 100 *Hypsilophodon* skeletons have been found on one Isle of Wight beach, Brighstone Bay.

English geologist Gideon Mantell named *Iguanodon* in 1825—17 years before paleontologist Richard Owen coined the word "dinosaur."

The paleontologists who discovered *Leaellynasaura*, Thomas Rich and Patricia Vickers-Rich, named it after their daughter, Leaellyn.

Gasparinisaura was named after the Argentinian paleontologist Zulma Brandoni de Gasparini. Two members of her team discovered the dinosaur.

At least three species of *Parasaurolophus* have been identified. The first, *Parasaurolophus walkeri*, was discovered as long ago as 1920.

In the past, some paleontologists argued that *Lambeosaurus* was aquatic and that its crest acted as a snorkel!

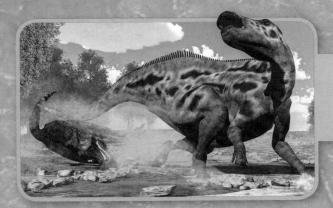

Shantungosaurus's femur (thighbone) was 5.6 feet (1.7 m) long.

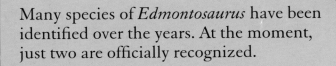

Many species of *Edmontosaurus* have been identified over the years. At the moment, just two are officially recognized.

The *Thescelosaurus* Willo contains organic, cell-like material. It could be from plants that it ate—or it could be from Willo itself.

Your Questions Answered

The main way that scientists find out fascinating facts about dinosaurs is that no matter how much they discover, it always leads them to ask new questions. With the help of incredible finds, as well as detailed research and new technologies, they are building up a more and more detailed picture of how dinosaurs used to live. Here are some fascinating questions paleontologists are now able to answer.

How did dinosaurs raise their young?

Dinosaurs laid eggs, just like birds and most reptiles do today. From the fossils that have been found, we know that at least some dinosaur species built nests, and also kept the eggs warm and protected from predators by brooding them. Once the young had hatched, they often remained with their parents.

Some fossilized eggs contain the remains of dinosaur embryos, which tells us a lot about how the animal grew and developed.

Which dinosaur was most common in the Cretaceous?

It is hard to know exact numbers of different dinosaur species, because our knowledge depends on the fossils that have been discovered. However, scientists believe that the Cretaceous saw huge numbers of some plant-eating dinosaurs, especially those that lived in herds. One example is *Iguanodon* (pages 10–11), which roamed many parts of Earth in large groups.

How do we know which dinosaur preyed on which?

Great white sharks can grow up to 20,000 teeth in their lifetime.

Like today's sharks, dinosaurs had teeth that continuously grew. When one tooth fell out, it was replaced by the next one. When predators attacked or ate their prey, this often resulted in loss of teeth. Many fossils of dinosaur carcasses also include teeth from meat-eating dinosaurs. While scientists cannot always be sure the owner of the teeth actually killed the prey, rather than just scavenging, it does tell us a lot about dinosaur food chains.

What do we know about prehistoric plants?

Paleontologists have discovered many fossilized plant parts—from tree barks and leaves to roots and cones—and have even been able to link some species to ones still alive today. So we know a lot about what plants looked like during different prehistoric periods, and where they grew. We also know which animals ate them, because sometimes the stomach contents of a dinosaur would fossilize along with the rest of its body, giving us an idea of its diet.

Scientists call the ginkgo tree a "living fossil," because its features have barely changed since prehistoric times.

How did dinosaurs communicate?

The most we know about dinosaur communication comes from studying hadrosaurs, such as *Parasaurolophus* (pages 16–17) and *Lambeosaurus* (pages 18–19). These dinosaurs had a crest on their head which scientists believe could have been key for their communication: it may have been used for display, to support hearing, to increase the animal's sense of smell, and to produce sounds that traveled particularly far. Rather than the roars we imagine dinosaurs produced, it's very likely that many made "closed-mouth" noises, like pigeons and ostriches do today.

Glossary

allosaur A large theropod with a long, narrow skull, usually with ornamental horns or crests.

ankylosaur A thyreophoran with defensive osteoderms and, sometimes, a tail club.

bipedal Walking upright on the back legs.

browse To feed on shoots, leaves, and other plant matter.

carnivore A meat-eater.

ceratopsian A marginocephalian with (usually) horns and frills. Early species were bipedal; later ones were large and quadrupedal.

Cretaceous period The time from 145 to 65 mya, and the third of the periods that make up the Mesozoic Era.

fossil The remains of an animal or plant that died long ago, preserved in rock.

gastrolith A stone in the stomach that helps digestion.

hadrosaur Also known as a duck-billed dinosaur, an ornithopod with an especially beak-like mouth.

herbivore A plant-eater.

iguanodontid A large, plant-eating ornithopod.

Jurassic period The time from 206 to 145 mya, and the second of the periods that make up the Mesozoic Era.

Mesozoic Era The period of geological time from 251 to 65 million years ago.

mya Short for "millions of years ago."

omnivore An animal that eats plants and meat.

ornithischian Describes dinosaurs with hip bones arranged like a bird's. All plant-eaters, they include ornithopods, marginocephalians, and thyreophorans.

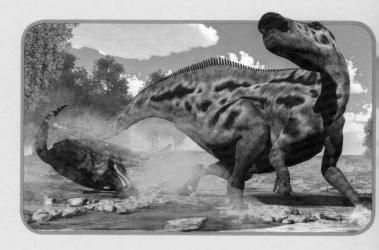

ornithopod An ornithischian dinosaur with a bony, beak-like mouth.

pachycephalosaur A bipedal marginocephalian with a thick skull.

paleontologist A scientist who studies fossils.

predator An animal that hunts and eats other animals for food.

quadrupedal Walking on all four legs.

sauropod An enormous, long-necked, plant-eating saurischian dinosaur that walked on all fours.

scavenge To eat carrion or leftover kills from other hunters.

species One particular type of living thing. Members of the same species look similar and can produce offspring together.

theropod A bipedal saurischian dinosaur with sharp teeth and claws.

Triassic period The time from 251 to 206 mya, and the first of the periods that make up the Mesozoic Era.

tyrannosaur A large theropod with a huge head and relatively small arms.

Further Information

BOOKS

Hulick, Kathryn. *The Science of Dinosaurs.* Minneapolis, MN: Abdo Publishing, 2017.

Miles, Liz. *Dinosaur Record Breakers.* New York, NY: Gareth Stevens Publishing, 2016.

Rissman, Rebecca. *Edmontosaurus and Other Duckbilled Dinosaurs: The Need-to-Know Facts.* North Mankato, MN: Capstone Press, 2017.

West, David. *Duck-Billed Dinosaurs.* New York, NY: Windmill Books, 2016.

Woolley, Katie. *Plant-Eating Dinosaurs.* New York, NY: Windmill Books, 2017.

WEBSITES

discoverykids.com/category/dinosaurs/
This Discovery Kids site has tons of awesome information about dinosaurs, plus lots of fun games and exciting videos!

kids.nationalgeographic.com/explore/nature/dinosaurs/
Check out this National Geographic Kids site to learn more about dinosaurs.

www.amnh.org/explore/ology/paleontology
This website by the American Museum for Natural History is filled with dinosaur quizzes, information, and activities!

Index